Prisons We Choose to Live Inside

DORIS LESSING

PRISONS WE CHOOSE TO LIVE INSIDE

CBC MASSEY LECTURES

Copyright © 1986 by Doris Lessing

Published in 1991 by
House of Anansi Press Limited
1800 Steeles Avenue West
Concord, Ontario
L4K 2P3

First published by CBC Enterprises in 1986

CBC logo used by permission

Canadian Cataloguing in Publication Data

Lessing, Doris, 1919-
Prisons we choose to live inside

Reprint. Originally published: Toronto: CBC Enterprises, 1986.
(CBC Massey lectures; 1985)

ISBN 0-88784-521-5

1. Social groups. 2. Individuality. 3. Responsibility.
I. Title. II. Series: CBC Massey lectures series; 1985.

HM251.L47   1991   302 C92-093050-6

Contents

The Massey Lectures Series

The Massey Lectures are co-sponsored by Massey College, in the University of Toronto, and CBC Radio. The series was created in honor of the Rt. Hon. Vincent Massey, former governor-general of Canada, and was inaugurated in 1961 to enable distinguished authorities to communicate the results of original study or research on important subjects of contemporary interest.

This book is based on the five-part Massey Lectures of the same name, which were broadcast in October 1985 as part of CBC Radio's "Ideas" series. Producer of the series was Damiano Pietropaolo; Executive Producer was Bernie Lucht.

The Author

With the 1950 publication of *The Grass is Singing*, Doris Lessing established herself as a major novelist. She has since had more than thirty books published, including her five-volume Children of Violence series and a dozen stories about Africa, where she was raised. The isolation of her parents' Southern Rhodesian farm was stifling to the young Lessing, and she learned to use her imagination to create her own fictional worlds. She quit school at age fourteen, continuing her education informally by extensive reading, particularly of American and English literature. When she was eighteen, Lessing moved to Salisbury, where she forged links that eventually led to her brief association with the Communist Party. In 1949, in her early twenties, she took Peter, her son from her second marriage, to England. Life in a seedy but colourful working-class section of London may have later inspired her wryly humorous *In Pursuit of the English*.

Lifelong observations of racial prejudice and sociopolitical oppression have shaped, in large part, Lessing's thematic considerations throughout her works. As a writer she reflects the human condition not so much in personal terms but in the broader social context, and her stories are distinguished by a strong concern for, as she puts it, "the individual conscience in its relation with the collective." Her literary explorations have taken her from social realism to, in more recent years, the somewhat fantastic realms of outer space and the inner space of the mind. Always progressive, Lessing is one of the most visionary and insightful writers of modern times.

When in the Future
They Look Back on Us

There was once a highly respected and prosperous farmer, who had one of the best dairy herds in the country, and to whom other farmers came from all over the southern half of the continent for advice. This was in the old Southern Rhodesia, now Zimbabwe, where I grew up. The time was just after the Second World War.

I knew this farmer and his family well. The farmer, who was Scotch by origin, decided to import a very special bull from Scotland. This was just before science had discovered how to send potential calves from one continent to another by airmail in small packages. The beast in due course arrived, flown in, naturally, and was welcomed by a reception committee of farmers, friends, experts. He cost £10,000. I don't know what that would be now, but it was a very large sum for the farmer. A special home was made for him. He was a massive, impressive animal, mild as a lamb, it was claimed, and he liked to be tickled at the back of his head with a stick held safely at a distance, from behind the bars of his pen. He had his own keeper, a black boy of about twelve. All went well; it was clear the bull would soon become the father of a satisfactory number of calves. He remained an attraction for visitors, who would drive out on a Sunday afternoon to stand about the pen, brooding over this fabulous beast, who looked so powerful and who was so docile. And then he suddenly and quite inexplicably killed his keeper, the black boy.

Something like a court of justice was held. The boy's relatives demanded, and got, compensation. But that was not the end of it. The farmer decided that the bull must be killed. When this became known, a great many people went to him and pleaded for the magnificent beast's life. After all, it was in the nature of bulls to suddenly go berserk, everyone knew that. The herd boy had been warned, and he must have been careless. Obviously, it would never happen again ... to waste all that power, potential, and not to mention money—what for?

"The bull has killed, the bull is a murderer, and he must be punished. An eye for an eye, a tooth for a tooth," said the inexorable farmer, and the bull was duly executed by firing squad and buried.

Now, as I've said, this farmer was not some ignoramus, or bumpkin. Moreover, like all his kind—the ruling white minority—he spent a good deal of time condemning the blacks who lived all around him for being primitive, backward, pagan, and so forth.

But what he had done—this act of condemning an animal to death for wrong-doing—went back into the far past of mankind, so far back we don't know where it began, but certainly it was when man hardly knew how to differentiate between humans and beasts.

Any tactful suggestions along these lines from friends or from other farmers were simply dismissed with: "I know how to tell right from wrong, thank you very much."

There is an other incident. A certain tree was once sentenced to death, at the end of the last war. The tree was associated with General Petain, for a time considered France's saviour, then France's betrayer. When Petain was disgraced, the tree was solemnly sentenced and executed for collaborating with the enemy.

I often think about these incidents: they represent those happenings that seem to give up more meaning as time goes on. Whenever things seem to be going along quite smoothly—and I am talking about human affairs in general—then it is as if suddenly some awful primitivism surges up and people revert to barbaric behaviour.

This is what I want to talk about in these five lectures: how often and how much we are dominated by our savage past, as individuals and as groups. And yet, while sometimes it seems as if we are helpless, we are gathering, and very rapidly—too rapidly to assimilate it—knowledge about ourselves, not only as individuals, but as groups, nations, and as members of society.

This is a time when it is frightening to be alive, when it is hard to think of human beings as rational creatures. Everywhere we look we see brutality, stupidity, until it seems that there is nothing else to be seen but that—a descent into barbarism, everywhere, which we are unable to check. But I think that while it is true there is a general worsening, it is precisely because things are so frightening we become hypnotized, and do not notice—or if we notice, belittle—equally strong forces on the other side, the forces, in short, of reason, sanity and civilization.

And of course I know that as I say these words there must be people who are muttering, "Where? The woman must be crazy to see anything good in this mess we are in."

I think this sanity must be looked for in precisely this process of judging our own behaviour—as we examine the farmer who executed an animal to make it expiate a crime, or the people who sentenced, and executed, a tree. Against these enormously powerful primitive instincts, we have this: the ability to observe ourselves from other viewpoints. Some of these viewpoints are very old—much older perhaps than we realize. There is nothing new in the demand that reason should govern human affairs. For instance, in the course of another study, I came upon an Indian book, a good two thousand years old, a manual for the sensible governing of a state. Its prescriptions are every bit as cool, sensible, rational as anything we could come up with now; nor does it demand any less in the way of justice, even as we understand justice. But the reason I am mentioning this book at all—it is called the *Arthâsàstra*, by the way, and was written by one Kautilya, and is unfortunately hard to come by out of specialist libraries—is that this book that seems so unimaginably old talks of itself as the last in a long line of similar books.

It could be said that this is a matter for gloom rather than optimism, that after so many thousands of years of knowing perfectly well how a country should be managed, we are so far from achieving it; but—and this is the whole point and focus of what I want to say—what we know about ourselves is much more sophisticated, goes deeper, than what was known then, what has been known through these long thousands of years.

If we were to put into practice what we know . . . but that is the point.

I think when people look back at our time, they will be amazed at one thing more than any other. It is this—that we do know more about ourselves now than people did in the past. But that very little of it has been put into effect. There has been this great explosion of information about ourselves. The information is the result of mankind's still infant ability to look at itself objectively. It concerns our behaviour patterns. The sciences in question are sometimes called the behavioural sciences and are about how we function in groups and as individuals, not about how we like to think we behave and function, which is often very flattering. But about how we can be observed to be behaving when observed as dispassionately as when we observe the behaviour of other species. These social or behavioural sciences are precisely the result of our capacity to be detached and unflattering about ourselves. There is this great mass of new information from universities, research institutions and from gifted amateurs, but our ways of governing ourselves haven't changed.

Our left hand does not know—does not want to know—what our right hand does.

This is what I think is the most extraordinary thing there is to be seen about us, as a species, now. And people to come will marvel at it, as we marvel at the blindness and inflexibility of our ancestors.

I spend a good deal of time wondering how we will seem to the people who come after us. This is not an idle interest, but a deliberate attempt to strengthen the power of that "other eye," which we can use to judge ourselves. Anyone who reads history at all knows that the passionate and powerful convictions of one century usually seem absurd, extraordinary, to the next. There is no epoch in history that seems to us as it must have to the people who lived through it. What we live through, in any age, is the effect on us of mass emotions and of social conditions from which it is almost impossible to detach ourselves. Often the mass emotions are those which seem the noblest, best and most beautiful. And yet, inside a year, five years, a decade, five decades, people will be asking, "How *could* they have believed that?" because events will have taken place that will have banished the said mass emotions to the dustbin of history. To coin a phrase.

People of my age have lived through several of such violent reversals. I will mention just one. During the Second World War, from the moment the Soviet Union was invaded by Hitler and became an ally of the democracies, that country was affectionately regarded in popular opinion. Stalin was Uncle Joe, the ordinary chap's friend,

Russia was the land of brave, liberty-loving heroes, and communism was an interesting manifestation of popular will—which we should copy. All this went on for four years and then suddenly, almost overnight, it went into reverse. All these attitudes became wrong-headed, treasonable, a threat to everybody. People who had been chatting on about Uncle Joe, suddenly, just as if all that had never happened, were using the slogans of the cold war. One extreme, sentimental and silly, bred by wartime necessities, was replaced by another extreme, un-reasoning and silly.

To have lived through such a reversal once is enough to make you critical for ever afterwards of current popular attitudes.

I think writers are by nature more easily able to achieve this detachment from mass emotions and social conditions. People who are continually examining and observing become critics of what they examine and observe. Look at all those utopias written through the centuries. More's *Utopia*, Campanella's *City of the Sun*, Morris's *News from Nowhere*, Butler's *Erewhon* (which is "no-where" backwards), all the many different blueprints for possible futures produced by science and space fiction writers who, I think, are in the same tradition. These of course are all criticisms of current societies, for you can't write a utopia in a vacuum.

I think novelists perform many useful tasks for their fellow citizens, but one of the most valuable is this: to enable us to see ourselves as others see us.

Of course in totalitarian societies writers are dis-trusted for precisely this reason. In all Communist countries this function, the criticizing one, is not permitted.

Incidentally, I see writers, generally, in every country, as a unity, almost like an organism, which has been evolved by society as a means of examining itself. This "organism" is different in different epochs and always changing. Its most recent evolution has been into space and science fiction, predictably, because humanity is "into" studying space, and has only recently (historically speaking) acquired science as an aptitude. The organism must be expected to develop, to change, as society does. The organism is not conscious of itself as an organism, a whole, though I think it will soon be. The world is becoming one, and this enables us all to see our many different societies as aspects of a whole, and the parts of those societies shared by them all. If you see writers like this—as a stratum, a layer, a strand, in every country, all so varied, but as together making up a whole, it tends to do away with the frantic competitiveness that is fostered by prizes and so forth. I think that writers everywhere are aspects of each other, aspects of a function that has been evolved by society.

Writers, books, novels, are *used* like this, but I don't think the attitudes towards writers, literature, reflect this. Not yet.

Novels should be on the same shelf with anthopology, says one friend of mine, an anthropologist. Writers comment on the human condition, talk about it continually. It is our subject. Literature is one of the most useful ways we have of achieving this "other eye," this detached manner of seeing ourselves; history is another. Yet literature and history increasingly are not seen like this by the young, as indispensible tools for living . . . but I'll come back to this later.

To return to the farmer and his bull. It may be argued that the farmer's sudden regression to primitivism affected no one but himself and his family, and was a very small incident on the stage of human affairs. But exactly the same can be seen in large events, affecting hundreds or even millions of people. For instance, when British and Italian soccer fans recently rioted in Brussels, they became, as onlookers and commentators continually reiterated, nothing but animals. The British louts, it seems, were urinating on the corpses of people they had killed. To use the word "animal" here seems to me unhelpful. This may be animal behaviour, I don't know, but it is certainly human behaviour, when humans allow themselves to revert to barbarism, and has been for thousands, probably even millions of years—depending on where one decides to put the beginning of our history as humans, not animals.

In times of war, as everyone knows who has lived through one, or talked to soldiers when they are allowing themselves to remember the truth, and not the sentimentalities with which we all shield ourselves from the horrors of which we are capable ... in times of war we revert, as a species, to the past, and are permitted to be brutal and cruel.

It is for this reason, and of course others, that a great many people enjoy war. But this is one of the facts about war that is not often talked about.

I think it is sentimental to discuss the subject of war, or peace, without acknowledging that a great many people enjoy war—not only the idea of it, but the fighting itself. In my time I have sat through many many hours listening to people talking about war, the prevention of war, the awfulness of war, with it never once being mentioned that for large numbers of people the idea of war is exciting, and that when a war is over they may say it was the best time in their lives. This may be true even of people whose experiences in war were terrible, and which ruined their lives. People who have lived through a war know that as it approaches, an at first secret, unacknowledged, elation begins, as if an almost inaudible drum is beating ... an awful, illicit, violent excitement is abroad. Then the elation becomes too strong to be ignored or overlooked: then everyone is possessed by it.

Before the First World War, the socialist movements of

all Europe and America met to agree that capitalism was fomenting war, and that the working classes of all those countries would have nothing to do with it. But the moment war was actually there, and the poisonous, fascinating elation had begun, all those decent, rational, honourable resolutions about keeping out of the war were forgotten. I have heard young people discussing this, uncomprehending. This is because they do not understand how it can have happened. It is because they have not experienced, and have not been told about that dreadful public elation that is so strong—strong because it comes from an older part of the human brain, of the human experience, than the decent, humane, rational part, which passes resolutions condemning war. But suppose the delegates to that socialists' conference had had such information. Even more importantly, suppose they had been prepared to discuss it as it affected them, for it is easy to call other people primitive, and difficult to acknowledge that we may be. Surely they would have been very much more efficient; indeed, as they had all expected, vainly, to happen, the working masses of Europe might have refused to go like lambs to the slaughter.

When I was in Zimbabwe recently, two years after Independence, and the end of that appalling war that was very much uglier and more savage than we were ever told, I met soldiers from both sides, whites and blacks. The first obvious fact—obvious to an outsider, if not to themselves—was that they were in a state of shock. Seven years of war had left them in a stunned, curiously blank state, and I think it was because whenever people are actually forced to recognize, from real experience, what we are capable of, it is so shocking that we can't take it in easily. Or take it in at all; we want to forget it. But there was another fact and for the purposes of this discussion perhaps a more interesting one. It was evident that the actual combatants on both sides, both blacks and whites, had thoroughly enjoyed the war. It was a fighting that demanded great skill, individual bravery, initiative, resourcefulness—the skills of a guerrilla, talents that through a long peace-time life may never have been called into use. Yet people may suspect they have them, and secretly long for an opportunity to show them. This is not the least of the reasons, I believe, that wars happen.

These people, black and white, men and women, had been living in that extreme of tension, alertness, danger, with all their capacities in full use. I heard people say that nothing could ever come up to that experience. The dreadfulness of the war was too near for them to be saying: "The best time of our lives," but they were, I am sure, beginning to think it. I am talking of course of the actual combatants, certainly not the civilians, who had a miserable time of it, with both the white government troops and the black guerrillas making use of them for their own purposes, treating them brutally.

By now, four years after, that war has gone away into the past, and has become formalized in sets of words, images of heroism. The young people will probably have a small unconscious hankering after what they hear in their parents' voices as they talk about it, if they were soldiers, that is. The civilians who lived through it will not talk about it much, having learned the impossibility of conveying the awfulness of it. But the black soldiers, most of whom were taught war as they came out of childhood, and the white soldiers, will be talking with nostalgia. The great war of liberation, the glorious war, which did so much psychological damage to the country, and to its people, damage which, after a war, we simply do not want to look at. Perhaps we *cannot* look at it, precisely as a result of that damage. This heroic and glorious war was quite unnecessary in the first place and could easily have been avoided by the use of only a minimum amount of common sense on the part of the whites. They were, however, in the grip of all kinds of primitive emotions. "I shall pick up my rifle and fight to the last drop of my blood." I quote. I go on to quote the first half of this sentence: "If you think that Reds like yourself and the British Government are going to give our country to the blacks, I shall pick up my rifle and fight to the last drop of my blood." And he did.

I heard precisely this sentiment recently from a white South African.

Yes, indeed it does seem that against passions as primitive as these, the small voice of reason is not likely to succeed. Let us look at South Africa, where the experiences of Kenya and white Rhodesia have taught them nothing. But perhaps, and we must hope it, tucked away among the fanatics are reasonable men and women who have taken a long cool look at Kenya and Rhodesia and learned. Perhaps. It does not look like it now.

This word "blood." It is always being used by leaders to raise our temperatures.

"The tree of liberty must be refreshed from time to time with the blood of patriots and tyrants. It is its natural manure." That is Thomas Jefferson.

"The blood shed by our soldiers will inspire us in the time of peace."

"Only through blood can we be reborn!"

"The way to a glorious future lies through blood."

"The blood of our martyrs shall be our inspiration: never shall we forget the blood that has been shed for us all."

It is not too much to say that when the word blood is pronounced, this is a sign that reason is about to depart.

All this blood business of course goes back to ritual sacrifice, the thousands of years during which priests slit the throats of first humans, then animals, to let blood flow out to please some savage diety. It goes very deep in us all, blood sacrifice, the sacrificial victims, scapegoats. When a leader invokes blood to arouse us to support him and his cause, it is time for us to be on our guard, to think of those long millenia when our ancestors' lives were safeguarded by blood and sacrifice. But our lives do not need blood; we only regress to the use of it when we are forced to. To reflect that it is nearly always those leaders who claim to be in the forefront of progress, enlightenment, etc. who are the most ready to invoke blood, does offer the pleasures of irony. Well—the pleasures of irony, one sometimes has to think, are the only consolation when contemplating the human story. . . .

"We will drown the Enemy in seas of his own blood."

Ah yes, the enemy. . . .

There was not long ago, a very interesting experiment in a certain American university. This was in a small university, near a small town, which had close ties with the university.

One day, representatives of the psychology department invited the townspeople to come up to the university campus and take part in an experiment. It was a nice day, the university was a pretty place, townspeople and university people were used to trying to please each other, and several hundred people arrived at the campus of the university at the time appointed. And then . . . nothing whatever happened. Nothing. The psychologists were nowhere to be seen. No explanations. No announcements. The visitors stood about waiting. Then they began to seek out acquaintances and friends, and still nothing happened. Discussing this, that they had all come up and nothing further was offered to them, they began to argue. Quite soon, there were two camps among them, with strongly opposing views. Next, the crowd had separated into two, and spokespeople had emerged. Debates ensued. Then quarrels. Much more was being discussed than the question of their being invited up here to their university (the townspeople thought of it as theirs) and then ignored. All kinds of issues were being aired and disagreed upon.

Past causes of disagreement emerged and took on a new life. It was being said that this occasion was turning out quite useful after all, because this was an opportunity to "have it out once and for all," as one woman put it. The two camps began to quarrel quite violently. Small scuffles began, first among the young men. At that point, when it was obvious that more serious fighting would begin, the psychologists appeared and said that as they had explained right from the beginning, this was a social experiment. Research was going on into the tendency of the human mind to see things in pairs—either/or, black/white, I and you, we and you, good and bad. The forces of good, the forces of evil.

"You, the crowd," went on these intrepid researchers, "have only been here for a couple of hours and already you are separated into two camps, with leaders, and each side sees itself as a repository of all good, and the other camp as at the best wrong-headed. And you were on the point of fighting about absolutely non-existent differences."

How that particular afternoon ended, we do not know, but I hope it was in a large jamboree of some kind, where all these artificially inflamed passions disappeared in harmony and good will.

This business of seeing ourselves as in the right, others in the wrong; our cause as right, theirs as wrong; our ideas as correct, theirs as nonsense, if not as downright evil. . . . Well, in our sober moments, our human moments, the times when we think, reflect, and allow our rational minds to dominate us, we all of us suspect that this "I am right, you are wrong" is, quite simply, nonsense. All history, development goes on through interaction and mutual influence, and even the most violent extremes of thought, of behaviour, become woven into the general texture of human life, as one strand of it. This process can be seen over and over again in history. In fact, it is as if what is real in human development—the main current of social evolution—cannot tolerate extremes, so it seeks to expel extremes and extremists, or to get rid of them by absorbing them into the general stream.

"All things are a flowing . . . ," as Heraclitus, the old Greek philosopher said.

There is no such thing as my being in the right, my side being in the right, because within a generation or two, my present way of thinking is bound to be found perhaps faintly ludicrous, perhaps quite outmoded by new development—at the best, something that has been changed, all passion spent, into a small part of a great process, a development.

You Are Damned, We Are Saved

I was brought up in a country where a small white minority dominated the black majority. In old Southern Rhodesia the white attitudes towards the blacks were extreme: prejudiced, ugly, ignorant. More to the point, these attitudes were assumed to be unchallengeable and unalterable, though the merest glance at history would have told them (and many of them were educated people) that it was inevitable their rule would pass, that their certitudes were temporary. But it was not permissible for any member of this white minority to disagree with them. Anybody who did faced immediate ostracism; they had to change their minds, shut up, or get out. While the white regime lasted—ninety years, which is nothing in historical terms—a dissident was a heretic and traitor. Also, the rules of this particular game demanded that it was not enough to say: "So and so disagrees with us, who are the possessors of evident truth." It had to also be said: "So and so is evil, corrupt, sexually depraved," and so on.

A few months after the start of the miners' strike in Britain, in 1984, just when it was moving into its second, more violent phase, a miner's wife came on television to tell her story. Her husband had been on strike for months and they had no money. While he supported the union, and agreed there should have been a strike, he thought Arthur Scargill had led the strike badly. Any-way, along with a minority, he had gone back to work. A gang of miners had broken this couple's windows, smashed up the inside of their house, and beaten up the man. The woman said she knew who these men were. It was a very tight community, she said. She recognized them. They were friends. She was stunned and bewil-dered. She could not believe that decent mining folk could have done such a thing. She said that one of these men who had been in the gang greeted her when he was alone, "just as he always had done," but when he was with his friends, she was invisible to him.

She simply could not understand it, she said. But I think—and this is absolutely my point, the point of these talks—that not only should she have understood it, she should have expected it; that we should all understand and expect these things, and build what we know from history and from the laws of society we already have into how we structure our institutions.

Of course it may be argued that this is a fairly bleak view of life. It means, for instance, that we can stand in a room full of dear friends, knowing that nine-tenths of them, if the pack demands it, will become your enemies—will, as it were, throw stones through your window. It means that if you are a member of a close-knit commu-nity, you know you differ from this community's ideas at the risk of being seen as a no-goodnik, a criminal, an evil-doer. This is an absolutely automatic process; nearly everyone in such situations behaves automatically.

But there is always the minority who do not, and it seems to me that our future, the future of everybody, depends on this minority. And that we should be think-ing of ways to educate our children to strengthen this minority and not, as we mostly do now, to revere the pack.

Bleak? Yes it is. But as we all know, growing up is

difficult and painful; and what we are talking about is the growing up of ourselves as social animals. Adults who hold on to all kinds of cosy illusions and comforting notions remain immature. The same holds good of us as groups or as members of groups—group animals.

It is easy for me now to say "group animal" or "the social animal." It is commonplace now to say we human beings were animals, and a great deal of our behaviour is rooted in past animal behaviour. This way of thinking has come about in a quiet revolution over the past, let us say, thirty or forty years. It is an interesting contradiction that while this revolution has gone on and has succeeded, on the whole it has been without the approval of the academics in the various fields. The popularizers are disapproved of, but that is nothing new. The professionals, the possessors of a certain field of knowledge, never like it when mavericks among themselves share it with the mob.

Something else contradictory is going on, and in those fields that are known as "the soft sciences"—psychology, sociology, social psychology, social anthropology and so on—precisely those areas where so many fascinating discoveries are being made about ourselves. It is the fashion to denigrate them, to call them the "failed" sciences. One constantly finds contemptuous or dismissive references to these "failed" disciplines. These departments are the first to be got rid of when retrenchments are being made. But what is interesting is that these are all new areas of study, very new, some of them less than half a century old. Looked at collectively they amount to a completely new attitude towards ourselves, our institutions—the detached, curious, patient, investigative attitude that I think is the most valuable thing we have in the fight against our own savagery, our long history as group animals. An enormous amount of work is being done, large numbers of experiments have been, are being, made, some of which transform our ideas about ourselves, and there are whole libraries full of a new type of book—completely new, the result of a new type of research.

As I said in the last lecture, I believe that people coming after us will marvel that on the one hand we accumulated more and more information about our behaviour, while on the other, we made no attempt at all to use it to improve our lives.

As an example, let us take what we know about how we function in groups. People in groups we now know are likely to behave in fairly stereotyped ways that are predictable. Yet when citizens join together to set up, let us say, a society for the protection of the unicorn, they do not say, this organism we're setting up is likely to develop in one of several ways. Let us take this into account and watch how we behave so that we control the society and the society does not control us. As another example, the Left might find it useful to say something like this: "It has been easily observable for some time that groups like ours always split and then the two new groups become enemies equipped with leaders who hurl abuse at each other. If we remain aware of this apparently inbuilt drive that makes groups split and split again we may perhaps behave less mechanically." Mind you, it seems it is not enough to be aware of how things are likely to happen. It is said that those highly intelligent people who set up the Bolshevik party in London in, I think, 1905, said to each other: "Let us learn from the French Revolution and let us not split violently over points of doctrine and then start murdering each other." But this is exactly what happened. They were helpless in the grip of forces they themselves had helped let loose. They did not understand what was happening to them. We have more and more information that can, if we use it, help us understand what is happening to us in various situations.

Yet everywhere, among certain kinds of persons, this great new achievement is put down. Why? I think that in this case it is more than just older generations of academics resenting new attitudes. I think that what they have been unconsciously looking for, and failing to find, are certitudes and dogmas, proven recipes that can be applied to every situation.

People like certainties. More, they crave certainty, they seek certainty, and great resounding truths. They like to be part of some movement equipped with these truths and certainties, and if there are rebels and heretics, that is even more satisfying, because this structure is so deep in all of us.

I live in Britain, a country that is rapidly being polarized into extremes. It is frightening to be a part of it. It is the miners' strike that precipitated or made obvious a process that began, I believe, with the collapse and fragmentation of the Left. For a very long time in Britain we have had a balance of left and right, each side containing within itself a large range of different opinions. This balance has gone. The Left is a mass of small and large groups. This is a classical recipe for social disorder, even revolution.

The polarization can be seen not only in politics. Universities for instance. A friend of mine decided to study anthropology. She found she had no alternative but to listen to Marxist lectures—lectures based on Marxist attitudes. If you say that Marxism is no longer a unity but a series of little churches, each with its own dogmas, I agree; but there are certain attitudes in common. These are again largely unconscious. Some things are not discussed, or hardly mentioned. It is possible to sit through hours, days, of discussion about war, and never hear it mentioned that one of the causes of war is that people enjoy it, or enjoy the idea of it. So it is also that one may hear, or read, interminabilities about the problems of the Left, and never hear it said that the reason why the Left is in such trouble is that people have seen socialism in action in country after country and are terrified of it. The Soviet Union: a tyranny, where if you disagree you find yourself in a mental hospital, because by definition you must be mad; a country where it is reckoned twenty million people died from the excesses of Stalin. China, where between twenty or sixty million people (the figures vary according to source) were slaughtered in the Cultural Revolution and where the country's progress was set back, according to its own estimates, by a generation. Cuba . . . Ethiopia . . . Somalia . . . South Yemen . . . I could go on, but there is no need. No need, except for people actually inside the Left. There, as always in great mass movements, reign certain sentimental certitudes that are unchallenged and undiscussed. One is that socialists are better than non-socialists—morally better, that is—in spite of the fact that socialism has created the most monstrous tyrannies, has murdered millions. And still does. Another certitude is that all capitalists are bad, mean ill to the community, are brutal and corrupt. Another, that socialists are peaceful by nature. Another, that women are inherently more peaceable than men. History does not exactly bear this out.

But I am not only talking in these lectures about socialism, capitalism, Marxism, and so on, but about belief—structures of belief. The time we live in is being described as The Age of Belief. No, it is not the first time the world has been afflicted with one. . . . But let us return to the miners' strike, which was unfortunately so rich in incidents useful to my thesis.

When it began, things were fluid, talk was of settlement and negotiation. Months passed and attitudes hardened. From the start large numbers of miners kept working. These were not hated by the strikers as much as were the miners who were on strike and then went back to work. This is a classic psychological pattern. Opponents are never hated as much as former allies. By Christmastime, we were accustomed to seeing on the television representatives of the two sides arguing their case. According to one side it was the miners who were responsible for the violence, for the rioting, for the disorder. According to the miners, the police and the scabs were responsible. Each side had not one good thing to say about the other, each side was lying . . . and lying with a good conscience, for the end justifies the means. Most of the people watching knew that both sides were in the wrong, that both were responsible for the violence, that both were lying, and lying with a good conscience. Everyone knows that at such times as strikes, civil wars, wars, from the moment they start there will be tragedies of all kinds, if for no other reason than that the people in every society who enjoy thuggery come to the surface. But the point is, everyone knows this at such times except the people involved, who seem to the onlookers as if they are drunk or hypnotized or have lost their senses. Well, they have. They've become part of some great mass lunacy and while they are in it no individual judgement can be expected from them.

What they say is formalized in sets of attitudes that are absolutely predictable.

The miners talking about their colleagues who chose to return to work, for instance. With a concentration of vituperation you would never think possible (in ordinary times) they were described as scabs, scum, filth, rubbish, criminals. This was to be expected. But the interesting thing was how much of it was in religious language. The miners returning to work had "left the fold," should "return to the fold," will be forgiven if they did "return to the fold." The striking miners had a "divine right" to this or that. Their struggle had of course been sanctified by suffering, by sacrifices.

It is by now of course a cliché that political movements and religious movements behave alike. We all talk now about the "churches" of socialism. About the "dogmas" of Marxism, similar to those of religious bigots. But I wonder if this way of talking has become a means of *not thinking*. As things are, we can discuss political bigotry, extremism, mass movements and their behaviour interminably and never mention our religious history once, except in some sort of vague way such as "religions and political movements have much in common."

We forget—and the young people don't know since they don't read history—that we are heirs of two thousand years, more or less, of a most tyrannical regime, beside which Hitler, Stalinism, are babes. Not that modern tyrants have not learned from the churches, some consciously. About the time of the First World War, the churches lost their teeth and ceased to become the major influence on our Western societies. Now they are amiable, often orientated towards work that is indistinguishable from social and charitable work, infinitely divided, and while some of the sects are totalitarian, it is not possible for the Church—as was the case till only yesterday, historically speaking—to dominate a whole society as the sole arbiter of conduct and thought. But for two thousand years Europe was under a tyrant—the Christian church—which allowed no other way of thinking, cut off all influences from outside, did not hesitate to kill, extirpate, persecute, burn and torture in the name of God. To remember this history is not for the sake of keeping alive the memories of old tyrannies, but to recognize present tyranny, for these patterns are in us still. It would be strange if they were not.

It is these patterns that I believe we should study,

become conscious of, and recognize as they emerge in us and in the societies we live in.

To say that socialism is a form of religion or that nazism was a religion, fascism was a religion, or that modern Communists often use religious phraseology, is not going to help us much unless we understand exactly what the pattern is we must look for.

The most easily observed bequest of Christianity to socialist thinking and behaviour is of course its sectarianism. We all know that socialist sects hate each other more than the enemy, or attack each other as if they do; we all know that the more extreme the dogma, the more extreme the attack. Just as Christians spent centuries killing each other for the correct interpretation of a word, a phrase, a sentence from the Bible, so now socialist sects revile each other, judge each other. Nosing out and extirpating heresy is the first concern.

It is the heritage of the structure of Christian thought in us that we should study.

The Christian believes that he or she is in a vale of tears, a situation from which she or he needs to be rescued, or "redeemed." This "redemption" will be because of the voluntary sacrifice of a superior being who takes the sins of the world upon himself. There will be a future state of absolute perfection, where there will be no suffering, or sorrow. Before this state is reached, there will be an intermediate time of preparation and of suffering.

Communists and socialists believe that the system in which we live is evil, that capitalists and businessmen are wicked, at the best well meaning, that there is no way out of this except by total change, almost certainly violent—a revolution that will demand blood and sacrifices. Extremists and fanatics of the Right and the Left believe that this change will be accomplished by a leader, to whom extravagant homage is given. There will be a period after the change-over from one system to another of much adjustment and preparation and discomfort—you can't make an omelette without breaking eggs—but the people must be purged of their errors that stem from the past. And after this purgative period, there will ensue a time of absolute happiness and fulfilment, full socialism, full communism, when sin will cease to exist. This is the structure of Christian thinking and the structure of political thinking on the Left and of many political groups not on the Left, but who believe in violent and drastic change because all heretics and evil ones have to be hounded to their deaths or "re-educated."

Described like this, it sounds like a kind of lunacy—which it is. A lunacy of immense strength. When I was a young woman I went through a period of being a Communist. It was a conversion, apparently sudden, and total (though short-lived). Communism was in fact a germ or virus that had already been at work in me for a long time. In my case, it was because of my rejection of the repressive and unjust society of old white-dominated Africa. But the point I want to make here is another one: we were a group of about forty people at its height. None of us was a freak, or eccentric. We were all normal members of society, or had been, for this was the war, and some of these people were refugees. Taken as a whole, we were probably more lively, energetic, well-read than most. Yet for the space of about two years, while the group was still whole, before it split apart and vanished, we held as axioms certain items of faith that really could not be questioned. That, for instance, in a very short space of time, probably about ten years, that is, when the war was over and the world was restored to normality, everyone would recognize the blessings of communism, and the world would be Communist, and be without crime, race prejudice or sex prejudice. (I have to point out here that the Women's Movement of the sixties did not originate criticism of sexism.). We believed that everyone in the world would be living in harmony, love, plenty and peace. For ever.

This was insane. And yet we believed it. And yet such groups continually spring into existence everywhere, have periods when such beliefs are their diet, while they hate and persecute and revile anybody who does not agree with them. It is a process that goes on all the time and I think must go on, because the patterns of the past are so strong in us that criticism of a society and a desire to change it fall so easily into such patterns.

I believe that we are in the grip of something very powerful and very primitive, and that we have not begun to come to grips with it. To study it, yes, that goes on in a hundred universities. But to apply it—no.

Recently I met an old friend and asked, as we do, "How are things with you?" "Terrible," she said. "I don't know what to do. My youngest daughter—she's eighteen now —has completely changed. You know we were always a very happy family, and I'm afraid I was taking it all for granted, but all that's changed."

I was thinking: "Ah, of course, poor Anne has got an attack of revolutionary politics, that must be it." But my friend was going on: "She was always a bit religious, as you know, she was interested in these cults, but she's become a Born Again Christian. Overnight she changed. She lives at home with us but she will hardly speak to any of us. She hates me the worst. She spends all her time with her new friends, she thinks they are all marvellous, she sees them as saints. I think they are pretty ordinary, nothing to write home about, and two of them are obviously dotty. But they are saved, you see. We are not. We are bound for hell-fire, but they are going to paradise. They have a leader, I think he's just a power-lover, but she can't see it, she thinks he's a saint of some kind. When I ask her how she can treat us, her family, as if we are all dirt, she says that Jesus said to his mother, "Woman what have I to do with you?"

Well, there we are, the same pattern exactly.

Of course my friend knows, just as my parents hopefully believed, when I presented them with exactly the same you-are-damned, I-and-my-friends-are-saved pattern, that her daughter will "grow out of it." The Western world is full of people who've been through this experience of being, when young, a member of a group of raving bigots and lunatics, and have emerged from it. I would say that half the people I know in Britain come into this category. But in our case it was political, not religious. Remembering our time of total commitment to a set of dogmas that we now find pathetic, we tend to wear wry smiles.

Meanwhile, we observe later generations going through it and, knowing what we are capable of, fear for them. Perhaps it is not too much to say that in these violent times the kindest, wisest wish we have for the young must be: "We hope that your period of immersion in group lunacy, group self-righteousness, will not coincide with some period of your country's history when you can put your murderous and stupid ideas into practice.

"If you are lucky, you will emerge much enlarged by your experience of what you are capable of in the way of bigotry and intolerance. You will understand absolutely how sane people, in periods of public insanity, can murder, destroy, lie, swear black is white."

Switching Off
to See Dallas

During the Korean War, the United States Government was astounded to find that American soldiers were confessing to all kinds of crimes they had not committed. This was because of brain-washing techniques applied by the North Koreans. As a result of this, the United States began intensive research into brain-washing and indoctrination. This research has gone on ever since, and has provided an enormous mass of information about society and how it operates, which could, I believe, transform us, transform our lives, how we view ourselves. This bit of history has interesting facets: one is that one may see how governments of all kinds, and priesthoods, have used brain-washing techniques to control their subjects for thousands of years. It is interesting to speculate to what extent it was pragmatic, how much based on conscious expertise. But it was certainly a step up in social self-consciousness when a powerful modern government instructed its experts to investigate an area which until then had been dark, and secret—to investigate it as dispassionately as anthropologists are supposed to when they examine the habits of a primitive tribe.

I remember the Korean War well. It was a very horrible war, but has been so overshadowed by the Vietnam War that it is remembered very little, except when a television company decides to put on "M.A.S.H." again. It was also horrible because it happened so soon after World War II, a war which should have been enough, some people believed—foolishly, it turned out—to put the world off war for ever.

It was the height of the cold war. There was a lowering, ugly, paranoid atmosphere. Suddenly the Communists announced that the Americans were dropping material infected with disease germs on to their enemies, and committing other atrocities well beyond the level of atrocities licensed by war. Some people simply refused to believe it; some people believed it, instantly, without further examination. Some fell into a gloomy anxious state of suspended judgement, repeating as one has to do: "In war time the first casualty is truth." The trouble was, something was lacking. What was lacking was information. The information that we lacked, then, was about brain-washing techniques.

Now when I look back I am surprised by something that did not strike me at all at the time. It is this: there had been plenty of recent examples of brain-washing, for instance in the Show Trials in Russia in the thirties and in Czechoslovakia, where people confessed to quite ridiculous crimes. And one could have contemplated with benefit the long history of witch-hunting, when women confessed, often without torture, to crimes. But it was as if some jump in our understanding had not taken place; we were not able to put things together in a way that made sense. On the one hand there were all those American soldiers admitting to all kinds of horrors, on the other, it was not possible to believe the United States Government had ordered them, even though everybody is properly suspicious about what all governments are prepared to do in war-time. But we could not fit these facts together in a way that made sense: a jump forward in our understanding had not taken place.

It is this jump forward that to my mind is the most

powerful force in social evolution: a movement into greater objectivity, shown in the public sphere when the United States government ordered its servants to investigate brain-washing techniques, which by definition had to mean techniques sometimes used by itself.

Used often unconsciously and pragmatically.

We are all of us, to some degree or another, brain-washed by the society we live in. We are able to see this when we travel to another country, and are able to catch a glimpse of our own country with foreign eyes. There is nothing much we can do about this except to remember that it is so. Every one of us is part of the great comforting illusions, and part illusions, which every society uses to keep up its confidence in itself. These are hard to examine, and the best we can hope for is that a kindly friend from another culture will enable us to look at our culture with dispassionate eyes.

But while these great half-conscious, or unconscious, processes are hard to examine, it is easy to study brain-washing and indoctrination in smaller contexts, for they go on all the time. For instance, take the cults and sects that proliferate.

Brain-washing has three main pillars or processes, by now well understood. The first is tension, followed by relaxation. This one is used, for instance in the interrogation of prisoners, when the interrogator is alternatively harsh and tender—one moment a sadistic bully, the next a kind friend. The second is repetition—saying or singing the same thing over and over again. The third is the use of slogans—the reducing of complex ideas to simple sets of words. These three are used all the time by governments, armies, political parties, religious groups, religions —and always have been used. While I said before it is interesting to speculate to what an extent the use of these methods is unconscious, it is more to our point here to remember that there is a difference between some sergeant-major using these methods to break in raw recruits, because he is doing what his kind have always done, and some sophisticated operator knowing exactly what he is doing.

In a certain university, not a thousand miles from here, as they say in the fairy tales, there is a researcher who has discovered that he can take a true believer—let us say, a Christian Scientist, but it doesn't matter what—or let's say, a person who is sure the world is flat or that the world will end on Friday the 13th of next Leap Year, and using classical brain-washing techniques, turn this faithful one, first into a Seventh-Day Adventist, then into a Stalinist Communist, then into a Liberal, then into a feminist, then into a hard-line atheist. When all these changes have been accomplished, and they can be done in the space of a few days, and while this person is a feminist, Stalinist, convinced capitalist, that is what she or he is, absolutely and definitely and finally, and prepared to die for it. But when all these changes have been gone through, the hapless one is returned to his or her former faith, let us say, convinced that the world will end on Friday the 13th. His or her brief periods as atheist, capitalist, etc., are now regarded as the merest whimsies on the part of the researcher, and the present faith, whatever it happens to be, is the true one: anyone who does not believe that the world will end on Friday the 13th is at the best misguided, but probably a liar, wicked, morally disgusting, to be avoided.

The natural reaction of almost everyone hearing this particular bit of social research is to assert, silently or loudly: "Of course I would never succumb like that silly person, I would be immune." And, whether said aloud or silently or said at all, we can also hear the implicit: "Because my beliefs are the correct ones." But no, alas, alas for all of us, every one of us would succumb, that is unless we were suffering from certain types of schizophrenia. The more sane we are, the more likely we are to be converted. But we may comfort ourselves with this: that brain-washing is usually not permanent. It wears off. We may be brain-washed—by conscious or unconscious manipulators, or we may brain-wash ourselves (not uncommon, this)—but it usually wears off.

Meanwhile, for some people this experiment I have just described is like a dawn after a long night. The end of The Age of Belief is in sight—you'd think the whole world would have cried out in relief and hope. Soon, soon, we will have left behind The Age of Belief and its wars and tortures and hatred of another type of believer, soon we will all be free and, as all the philosophers and sages have recommended, we will all live our lives with minds free of violent and passionate commitment, but in a condition of intelligent doubt about ourselves and our lives, a state of quiet, tentative, dispassionate curiosity. What, *all* of us? Everybody? Including all those raging fanatics out there with their ridiculous ideas? All, all prepared to say: "It is the end of the Age of Faith; we will each one of us give up the flattering and comforting idea that we, only we, only I am in the right"?

Well, obviously a desire to believe in a Golden Age dies hard . . . and here am I with my version of it. But joking apart, it does seem to me that there is a new thing in the world, when even a few people can examine themselves so coolly.

If you want to investigate brain-washing in small doses, in small ways, then join one of the sects who will use, probably unconsciously, these brain-washing techniques. Of course you take the chance that you will fall victim to them. Instead of the attitude, "What a wonderful opportunity to examine this fascinating social process, you may suddenly find yourself crying, "At last, I've discovered the truth! This group of people I so coldly decided to investigate are the possessors of truth, they are my true family. They want me to become part of them, and I will, because I understand that all the people outside this family are lost souls, they are no good. They don't understand. They are scum, rubbish, but anyway I don't want to think about them at all. I need my own new family because the world is a terrible place, and the arena for unceasing struggle and conflict and a battle-ground between good and evil, God and the devil, (or Communists and capitalists) and my new friends and I will fight together on the side of the good. I must not be soft towards my own family and my former friends, because my first duty is to my new family, my real one, and they really care for me, they understand me, but my former family did not really love me and understand me. Besides, I need a whole-hearted and pure attitude because my new group, my allies, have so many enemies who want to destroy us, and I must be prepared to fight for what I believe in and kill if necessary. You can't make an omelette without breaking eggs and one day we will have a perfect, good, noble, free world, but only we—I and my new family and the people who believe in us—can create it."

If you have not succumbed to this—and a great many people have involuntarily submitted to the process, myself included—and if you think it's a bit risky, well, it is very easy to watch these processes at work in the hands of government and of course, by advertisers. Watch television adverts, for instance. . . .

Or how about the Falklands War? Let's discuss it without prejudice, never mind whether I agreed with it or not. I have friends who exclaim that the worst part of that war was watching our country suddenly reverting to what they described as outworn jingoism and simple-minded patriotism. Why outmoded? Any nation can be made to revert to drum-beating, to dancing around a campfire waving tomahawks—metaphorically speaking

—by any leader able to use the appropriate phrases and war cries. It occurs to me here to wonder that since it is so easy to arouse the primitive in a nation, which then may easily revere the leader for doing it, where are the leaders who instead choose to appeal to a nation's higher instincts? Who are they?

When Mrs. Thatcher was elected for her second term of office, she employed Saatchi & Saatchi, a big advertising firm, to handle her campaign. These people used every trick in the book, from turns of phrase calculated to arouse easy emotions, to the colours of her dresses and the curtains she stood in front of, to calculated entrances and exits and the use of the media. Meanwhile, her highminded socialist opposition despised these tricks, and the media. We were able to watch exactly how Mrs. Thatcher's campaign was stage managed, in a very witty, clever television programme. When I say "we" I mean a minority of the nation who watched it. But I would have been in favour of making it compulsory viewing.

We have now reached the stage where a political leader not only uses, skilfully, time-honoured rabble rousing tricks—see Shakespeare's Julius Caesar—but employs experts to make it all more effective. But the antidote is that, in an open society, we may also examine these tricks being used on us. If, that is, we choose to examine them; if we don't switch off to see Dallas or whatever instead.

The point I am making is that information we have been given about ourselves, as individuals, as groups, as crowds, as mobs, is being used consciously and deliberately by experts, which almost every government in the world now employs to manipulate its subjects. More and more we will be able to observe governments using the results of the research into brain-washing but only if we wish to observe, only if we are determined not to fall victim to them.

Meanwhile, it is interesting that those people who like

to regard themselves as the armies of the good, the well-intentioned, disdain such means. I am not saying they should use them, but they will often refuse even to study them, thus leaving themselves open to being manipulated by them. As an experiment I tried talking about this subject to a series of my friends who are part of the well-intentioned movements of our time, such as Greenpeace, various types of socialism, people against nuclear war, campaigners for civil liberties, for the rights of prisoners, the abolition of torture, and so on. Every one reacted identically—emotionally, with dislike and distrust, as if it were in some way reactionary or anti-libertarian or anti-democratic to look at the behaviour of human beings, at *our* behaviour, dispassionately, as something that one may learn to predict.

Our opponents have no such inhibitions.

Of course, if you are a member of a group that by its own definition is right, good and true, with all the complacent attitudes that go with this—such as that one's opponents are evil—then of course it is hard to stand aside, hard to take that necessary step upwards on the ladder into objectivity.

But it does seem to me sometimes that Thatcher's last election exactly summed it up: there she was, her every gesture, exit, entrance, smile, remark, stage managed according to very sophisticated social prescription; while Michael Foot was grumpily and highmindedly slamming a train window in the faces of some enquiring reporters.

We observe India's Rajiv Gandhi winning an election with the aid of a friend, a film star who is the idol of millions of people. To your south, a film star is the most popular president—I have heard said—of the century. It is not without a strong feeling of unreality that I've listened to people discussing why Reagan is so successful without it ever being mentioned that it is just possible that people may be voting for him because he has already, as it were, been elected at the box office.

Government by show business. . . . Well, every author-itarian government understands this very well. Think of Hitler's great mass demonstrations when millions of people were whipped up into hysteria, or the enormous military parades of the Soviet Union, using beautiful children, girls, dancing, flowers, songs . . . side by side with fear and threat.

Our new terrifying technologies go hand in hand with new psychological information.

And sometimes technology leads to unforeseen results. I have just been reading an account of how sol-diers destined for the front line are desensitized by delib-erately exposing them to brutality in such a way that they slowly lose their capacity for seeing the people they have to attack, or interrogate, as human. This is a con-trolled and skilled process where the trainers know ex-actly what they are doing, and how to take their charges slowly, stage by stage, until they can torture or kill with-out any emotion whatsoever.

There have been protests about this in various coun-tries, recently, but while I am sure no fewer soldiers are processed in this way, there is less noise about it. But what strikes me is this: technology—television, cinema, to be precise—in this case is doing exactly the same process, exposing us to brutality of every kind so that we lose our sensitivity to it. We lose our sensitivity in a random and unpredictable way.

Pictures from the Ethiopian famine roused the con-science of people in many countries. But pictures of vic-tims from another part of the world may not cause us to react. Not long ago we were told that a very large num-ber of people were to be publicly hanged in Nigeria, and there was practically no world response. Some of us remember, after World War II, the shock, the unease expressed around the world when the Soviet Union decided to publicly hang some German war criminals to appease the outrage of the plundered, pillaged and slaughtered Russian civilians. We were shocked, though we had been through nearly five years of horrors: we had supped and we were full of horrors, but not so full we could not still react. I wonder if anyone would protest now; we have become blunted. We have become desensitized. Watching, night after night, day after day, year after year, the horrors going on all over the world have desensitized us exactly as those soldiers have been deliberately brutalized. No one set out to brutalize us, to make us callous; but that is what we increasingly are.

This is not the result of some cynical expert manipulator deliberately using knowledge of psychology, but as an almost haphazard result of our technology.

I wonder if perhaps in the future people interested in these things will enquire, what was it that triggered world conscience about Ethiopia when the same conscience remained unmoved about the famine and suffering caused by the Soviet Union in Afghanistan? There are over five million refugees in Pakistan and Iran, over one third of its population. In Afghanistan crops are deliberately destroyed by napalm, villages ruined, children crippled by the use of explosives hidden in toys. It has been described as deliberate genocide in certain areas. A million civilians have been murdered. People die there as I write of starvation, yet there have been no great public campaigns over this. The world's heart has not been opened to the victims in Afghanistan where there is a Soviet puppet government; but the world's heart is open to Ethiopia, which is under a Soviet puppet government. People have been dying of famine along the countries of the Sahel for a decade or more but that trigger was not pulled, and people did not react with generosity and compassion, until recently. But why not? It is, at least, an interesting question to ask. . . .

Yet there will be people who think that to ask it is callous, or at the very least in bad taste.

It seems to me, more and more, that we are being governed by waves of mass emotion, and while they last it is not possible to ask cool, serious questions. One simply has to shut up and wait, everything passes. . . . But meanwhile, these cool, serious questions and their cool, serious, dispassionate answers could save us.

Looking back over my life, which has now lasted sixty-six years, what I see is a succession of great mass events, boilings up of emotion, of wild partisan passion, that pass, but while they last it is not possible to do more than think: "These slogans, or these accusations, these claims, these trumpetings, quite soon they will seem to everyone ridiculous and even shameful." Meanwhile, it is not possible to say so.

I was born as a result of the First World War, which shadowed my childhood. It was a war during which national emotions were primitive, vile, and so stupid that now young people can be heard enquiring: "But *how* could they have believed that? Why did they fight?"

The coming of the Second World War shadowed my growing up, and my two marriages were the result of this war—which was caused by a ranting and raving lunatic.

Communism boiled up in Russia, murdered and destroyed. Yet for a while the violent partisan passions of that revolution spread everywhere, and made it impossible to think straight. For some people in some places, it is still impossible to think straight.

China boiled up in revolution, boiled up again in the Cultural Revolution and set the country back a generation. But while these great social whirlpools, or earthquakes, or volcanoes, were at work, the people who were involved could not talk sense or ask questions or protest.

PRISONS WE CHOOSE TO LIVE INSIDE

One mass movement, each a set of mass opinions, succeeds another: for war, against war; against nuclear war; for technology, against technology. And each breeds a certain frame of mind: violent, emotional, partisan, always suppressing facts that don't suit it, lying, and making it impossible to talk in the cool, quiet, sensible low-keyed tone of voice which, it seems to me, is the only one that can produce truth.

And yet, while all these boilings and upheavals go on, at the same time, parallel, continues this other revolution: the quiet revolution, based on sober and accurate observation of ourselves, our behaviour, our capacities. In a thousand universities, laboratories, or in deliberately contrived research situations, information is being collected which could, if we decided to use it, transform the world we live in. But it means making that deliberate step into objectivity and away from wild emotionalism, deliberately choosing to see ourselves as, perhaps, a visitor from another planet might see us.

It means, and I hope that this won't sound too wild, choosing to laugh. . . . The researchers of brain-washing and indoctrination discovered that people who knew how to laugh resisted best. The Turks, for instance . . . the soldiers who faced their torturers with laughter sometimes survived when others did not. Fanatics don't laugh at themselves; laughter is by definition heretical, unless used cruelly, turned outwards against an opponent or enemy. Bigots can't laugh. True believers don't laugh. Their idea of laughter is a satirical cartoon pillorying an opposition person or idea. Tyrants and oppressors don't laugh at themselves, and don't tolerate laughter at themselves.

Laughter is a very powerful thing, and only the civilized, the liberated, the free person can laugh at herself, himself.

When the Shah of Iran was still on his throne, this

happened in a village in Persia. A certain quiet, law-abiding and sensible man called his beautiful and favourite cat, Shah-in-Shah, which is what the great kings of Persia have liked to be called—King of Kings. A village policeman, hearing of this, denounced the unfortunate man to the secret police and he was thrown into prison and vanished, as people did then and do now, of course, under Khomeini.... I have mentioned this incident to supporters of the old regime, only to be told that it was ridiculous, and the Shah himself would have thought so. Ah, but here we are up against a law of society that law givers don't take into account at all when they make our laws and then sit back, satisfied that the laws are just, and the society a good one. It is this: the people at the top of a government, a department, a ministry, or any institution of government or administration never know what goes on at the lower levels. This accounts for this scene, which is played out every day, all over the world, in every country, where some small citizen, who has been bullied or misgoverned or treated unjustly, listens incredulously while some great man or woman—the boss —announces that it is impossible that so and so could have happened under him, under his or her rule, for such a thing would be against the regulations and would never be tolerated by him or by her. How many times have you or I not sat and watched or listened, amazed, at this scene on television or radio. "No, certainly not, of course *my* policemen don't beat up helpless people in cells, frame the innocent; of course *my* officials don't bully helpless people or take bribes, of course such awful dreadful injustice such as you describe cannot happen." But it does, it just has. It is because, as I said above, people at the top don't know what goes on under them. Sometimes one cynically has to believe that they don't want to know.... At any rate, they are clearly helpless against this mechanism, which ensures that in every country I have lived in, visited, read about, people at the bottom of the heap are badly treated. Is it not possible for something to be done about this? Well, no, nothing can be done until we have reached that point where we can say that this *is* so, it will always be so, unless there are safeguards.

In some countries in the ancient times, there was a checking mechanism, set up by the kings who were the authorities of those days. There were government employees whose job it was to go about pretending to be ordinary citizens, to check the behaviour of officials. If an official was found to be stupid, or offensive, or bullying, or unjust, then he was removed. No official anywhere could ever be sure that the person standing in front of him, apparently helpless, was not a government inspector in disguise. And officials correspondently behaved with more care, and the standard of public service was kept high.

That device for improving administration could only have been employed if the administrations in question were able to look very coolly at themselves, and to diagnose their own condition, and to prescribe for it.

There is nothing to stop us doing the same.

Group Minds

People living in the West, in societies that we describe as Western, or as the free world, may be educated in many different ways, but they will all emerge with an idea about themselves that goes something like this: I am a citizen of a free society, and that means I am an individual, making individual choices. My mind is my own, my opinions are chosen by me, I am free to do as I will, and at the worst the pressures on me are economic, that is to say I may be too poor to do as I want.

This set of ideas may sound something like a caricature, but it is not so far off how we see ourselves. It is a portrait that may not have been acquired consciously, but is part of a general atmosphere or set of assumptions that influence our ideas about ourselves.

People in the West therefore may go through their entire lives never thinking to analyze this very flattering picture, and as a result are helpless against all kinds of pressures on them to conform in many kinds of ways.

The fact is that we all live our lives in groups—the family, work groups, social, religious and political groups. Very few people indeed are happy as solitaries, and they tend to be seen by their neighbours as peculiar or selfish or worse. Most people cannot stand being alone for long. They are always seeking groups to belong to, and if one group dissolves, they look for another. We are group animals still, and there is nothing wrong with that. But as I suggested in the last talk in this series, what is dangerous is not the belonging to a group, or groups, but not understanding the social laws that govern groups and govern us.

When we're in a group, we tend to think as that group does: we may even have joined the group to find "like-minded" people. But we also find our thinking changing because we belong to a group.

It is the hardest thing in the world to maintain an individual dissident opinion, as a member of a group.

It seems to me that this is something we have all experienced—something we take for granted, may never have thought about it. But a great deal of experiment has gone on among psychologists and sociologists on this very theme. If I describe an experiment or two, then anyone listening who may be a sociologist or psychologist will groan, oh God not *again*—for they will have heard of these classic experiments far too often. My guess is that the rest of the people will never have heard of these experiments, never have had these ideas presented to them. If my guess is true, then it aptly illustrates my general thesis, and the general idea behind these talks, that we (the human race) are now in possession of a great deal of hard information about ourselves, but we do not use it to improve our institutions and therefore our lives.

A typical test, or experiment, on this theme goes like this. A group of people are taken into the researcher's confidence. A minority of one, two, are left in the dark. Some situation demanding measurement or assessment is chosen. For instance, comparing lengths of wood that differ only a little from each other, but enough to be perceptible, or shapes that are almost the same size. The majority in the group—according to instruction—will assert stubbornly that these two shapes or lengths are the same length, or size, while the solitary individual, or the couple, who have not been so instructed will assert that the pieces of wood or whatever are different. But the majority will continue to insist—speaking metaphorically —that black is white, and after a period of exasperation, irritation, even anger, certainly incomprehension, the minority will fall into line. Not always, but nearly always. There are indeed glorious individualists who stubbornly insist on telling the truth as they see it, but most give in to the majority opinion, obey the atmosphere.

When put as baldly, as unflatteringly, as this, reactions tend to be incredulous: "I certainly wouldn't give in, I speak my mind...." But would you?

People who have experienced a lot of groups, who perhaps have observed their own behaviour, may agree that the hardest thing in the world is to stand out against one's group, a group of one's peers. Many agree that among one's most shameful memories are of saying that black is white because other people are saying it.

In other words, we know that this is true of human behaviour, but how do we know it? It is one thing to admit, in a vague uncomfortable sort of way (which probably includes the hope that one will never again be in such a testing situation) but quite another to make that cool step into a kind of objectivity, where one may say: "Right, if that's what human beings are like, myself included, then let's admit it, examine and organize our attitudes accordingly."

This mechanism, of obedience to the group, does not only mean obedience or submission to a small group, or one that is sharply determined, like a religion or political party. It means, too, conforming to those large vague, ill-defined collections of people who may never think of themselves as having a collective mind because they are aware of differences of opinion—but which, to people from outside, from another culture, seem very minor.

PRISONS WE CHOOSE TO LIVE INSIDE

The underlying assumptions and assertions that govern the group are never discussed, never challenged, probably never noticed, the main one being precisely this: that it *is* a group mind, intensely resistant to change, equipped with sacred assumptions about which there can be no discussion.

Since my field is literature, it is there I most easily find my examples. I live in London, and the literary community there would not think of itself as a collective mind, to put it mildly, but that is how I think of it. A few mechanisms are taken for granted enough to be quoted and expected. For instance, what is called "the ten-year rule," which is that usually when a writer dies, her or his work falls out of favour, or from notice, and then comes back again. It is one thing to think vaguely that this is likely to happen, but is it useful? Does it have to happen? Another very noticeable mechanism is the way a writer may fall out of favour for many years—while still alive, be hardly noticed—then suddenly be noticed and praised. An example is Jean Rhys, who lived for many years in the country. She was never mentioned, she might very well have been dead, and most people thought she was. She was in desperate need of friendship and help and did not get it for a long time. Then, due to the efforts of a perspicacious publisher, she finished *The Cruel Sargasso Sea*, and at once as it were became visible again. But—and this is my point—all her previous books, which had been unmentioned and unhonoured, were suddenly remembered and praised. Why were they not praised at all during that long period of neglect? Well, because the collective mind works like that—it is follow-my-leader, people all saying the same thing at the same time.

One can say of course that this is only "the way of the world." But does it have to be? If it does have to be, then at least we could expect it, understand it, and make allowances for it. Perhaps if it is a mechanism that is known to be one then it might be easier for reviewers to be braver and less like sheep in their pronouncements.

Do they have to be so afraid of peer group pressure? Do they really not see how they repeat what each other says?

One may watch how an idea or an opinion, even a phrase, springs up and is repeated in a hundred reviews, criticisms, conversations—and then vanishes. But meanwhile each individual who has bravely repeated this opinion or phrase has been the victim of a compulsion to be like everybody else that has never been analyzed—or not by her or by him. Though it is easily observable by outsiders.

This is of course the mechanism that journalists rely on when they visit a country. They know if they interview a small sample of a certain kind, or group, or class of people, these two or three citizens will represent all the others, since at any given time, all the people of any group or class or kind will be saying the same things, in the same words.

My experience as Jane Summers illustrates these and many other points. Unfortunately there isn't time here to tell the story properly. I wrote two books under another name, Jane Summers, which were submitted to publishers as if by an unknown author. I did this out of curiosity and to highlight certain aspects of the publishing machine. Also, the mechanisms that govern reviewing. The first, *The Diary of a Good Neighbour*, was turned down by my two main publishers. It was accepted by a third and also by three European publishers. The book was deliberately sent to all the people who regard themselves as experts of my work and they didn't recognize me. Eventually, it was reviewed, as most new novels are, briefly and often patronizingly, and would have vanished forever leaving behind a few fan letters. Because Jane Summers did get fan letters from Britain and the United

States, the few people in on the secret were amazed that no one guessed. Then I wrote the second, called *If the Old Could*, and still no one guessed. Now people keep saying to me: "How is it possible that no one guessed? I would have guessed at once." Well, perhaps. And perhaps we're all more dependent on brand names and on packaging than we'd like to think. Just before I came clean, I was asked by an interviewer in the States what I thought would happen. I said that the British literary establishment would be angry and say the books were no good, but that everyone else would be delighted. And this is exactly what happened. I got lots of congratulatory letters from writers and from readers who had enjoyed the joke—and very sour and bitchy reviews. However, in France and in Scandinavia the books came out like this: The Diaries of Jane Summers by Doris Lessing. I have seldom had as good reviews as I did in France and in Scandinavia for the Jane Summers books. Of course, one could conclude that the reviewers in France and Scandinavia have no taste but that the British reviewers have.

It has all been very entertaining but it has left me with the feeling, as well, of being sad and embarrassed for my profession. Does everything always have to be so predictable? Do people really have to be such sheep?

Of course, there are original minds, people who do take their own line, who do not fall victim to the need to say, or do, what everyone else does. But they are few. Very few. On them depends the health, the vitality of all our institutions, not only literature, from which I have been drawing my examples.

It has been noticed that there is this ten percent of the population, who can be called natural leaders, who do follow their own minds into decisions and choices. It has been noted to the extent that this fact has been incorporated into instructions for people who run prisons, concentration camps, prisoner of war camps: remove the ten percent, and your prisoners will become spineless and conforming.

Of course, we are back here with the notion of elitism, which is so unfashionable, so unlikeable to the extent that in large areas of politics, even education, the idea that some people may be naturally better equipped than others is resisted. But I will return to the subject of elitism later. Meanwhile, we may note that we all rely on, and we respect, this idea of the lonesome individualist who overturns conformity. It is the recurrent subject of archetypal American films—*Mr. Smith Goes To Washington*, for instance.

Take the way an attitude towards a certain writer or a book will be held by everyone, everyone saying the same things, whether for praise or for blame, until opinion shifts. This shift can be part of some wider social shift. Let us take the Women's Movement, as an example. In London there is a lively, courageous publisher called Virago, run by women. A great many women writers who have been ignored or not taken seriously have been re-evaluated by them. But sometimes the shift is because one person stands out against the prevailing tide of opinion, and the others fall into line behind him, or her, and the new attitude then becomes general.

This mechanism is of course used all the time by publishers. When a new writer, a new novel, has to be launched, the publisher will look for an established writer to praise it. Because one "name" says it is good, the literary editors take notice and the book is launched. It is easy to see this bit of machinery at work in oneself: if someone one respects says such and such a thing is good, when you think it isn't, it is hard to differ. If several people say it is good, then it is correspondently harder.

At a time when one set of attitudes is in the process of changing to another, it is easy to see the hedging-your-bets mechanism. A reviewer will write a piece nicely balanced between one possibility and another. A light, knowing, urbane tone often goes with this. This particular tone is used a great deal on radio and television, when doubtful subjects are under discussion. For example, when it was believed that it was impossible for us to put men on the moon, which is what the Astronomer Royal said a few years before we did. This light, mocking, dismissive tone divorces the speaker from the subject: he or she addresses the listener, the viewer, as if it were over the head of the stupid people who believe that we could put men on the moon, or that there may be monsters in Loch Ness or Lake Champlain, or that . . . but fill in your own pet possibility.

Once we have learned to see this mechanism in operation, it can be seen how little of life is free of it. Nearly all the pressures from outside are in terms of group beliefs, group needs, national needs, patriotism and the demands of local loyalties, such as to your city and local groups of all kinds. But more subtle and more demanding—more dangerous—are the pressures from inside, which demand that you should conform, and it is these that are the hardest to watch and to control. If possible.

Many years ago I visited the Soviet Union, during one of their periods of particularly severe literary censorship. The group of writers we met was saying that there was no need for their works to be censored, because they had developed what they called "inner censorship." That they said this with pride shocked us westerners. What was shocking was that they were so naive about it, cut off as they are from information about psychological and sociological development. This "inner censorship" is what the psychologists call "internalizing" an exterior pressure—such as a parent—and what happens is that a previously resisted and disliked attitude becomes your own.

This happens all the time, and it is often not easy for the victims themselves to know it.

There are other experiments done by psychologists and sociologists that underline that body of experience to which we give the folk-name, "human nature." They are recent; that is to say, done in the last twenty or thirty years. There have been some pioneering and key experiments that have given birth to many others along the same lines—as I said before, over-familiar to the professionals, unfamiliar to most people.

One is known as the Milgram experiment. I have chosen it precisely because it was and is controversial, because it was so much debated, because all the professionals in the field probably groan at the very sound of it. Yet, most ordinary people have never heard of it. If they did know about it, were familiar with the ideas behind it, then indeed we'd be getting somewhere. The Milgram experiment was prompted by curiosity into how it is that ordinary decent, kindly people, like you and me, will do abominable things when ordered to do them—like the innumerable officials under the Nazis who claimed as an excuse that they were "only obeying orders."

The researcher put into one room people chosen at random who were told that they were taking part in an experiment. A screen divided the room in such a way that they could hear but not see into the other part. In this second part volunteers sat apparently wired up to a machine that administered electric shocks of increasing severity up to the point of death, like the electric chair. This machine indicated to them how they had to respond to the shocks—with grunts, then groans, then screams, then pleas that the experiment should terminate. The person in the first half of the room believed the person in the second half was in fact connected to the machine. He was told that his or her job was to administer increasingly severe shocks according to the instructions of the experimenter and to ignore the cries of pain and pleas from the other side of the screen. Sixty-two percent of the people tested continued to administer shocks up to the 450 volts level. At the 285 volt level the guinea pig had given an agonized scream and become silent. The people administering what they believed were at the best extremely painful doses of electricity were under great stress, but went on doing it. Afterwards most couldn't believe they were capable of such behaviour. Some said: "Well I was only carrying out instructions."

This experiment, like the many others along the same lines, offers us the information that a majority of people, regardless of whether they are black or white, male or female, old or young, rich or poor, will carry out orders, no matter how savage and brutal the orders are. This obedience to authority, in short, is not a property of the Germans, under the Nazis, but a part of general human behaviour. People who have been in a political movement, at times of extreme tension, people who remember how they were at school, will know this anyway . . . but it is one thing carrying a burden of knowledge around, half conscious of it, perhaps ashamed of it, hoping it will go away if you don't look too hard, and another saying openly and calmly and sensibly: "Right. This is what we must expect under this and that set of conditions."

Can we imagine this being taught in school, imagine it being taught to children: "If you are in this or that type of situation, you will find yourself, if you are not careful, behaving like a brute and a savage if you are ordered to do it. Watch out for these situations. You must be on your guard against your own most primitive reactions and instincts."

Another range of experiments is concerned with how children learn best in school. Some results go flat against some of most cherished current assumptions such as, for instance, that they learn best not when "interested" or "stimulated" but when they are bored. But putting that aside—it is known that children learn best from teachers who expect them to learn well. And most will do badly if not much is expected from them. Now, we know that in classes of mixed boys and girls, most teachers will—quite unconsciously—spend more time on the boys than on the girls, expect much more in scope from the boys, will consistently underestimate the girls. In mixed classes, white teachers will—again quite unconsciously—denigrate the non-white children, expect less from them, spend less time on them. These facts, I say, are known—but where are they incorporated, where are they used in schools? In what town is it said to teachers something like this: "As teachers you must become aware of this, that attention is one of your most powerful teaching aids. Attention—the word we give to a certain quality of respect, an alert and heedful interest in a person—is what will feed and nourish your pupils." (To which of course I can already hear the response: "But what would you do if you had thirty children in your class, how much attention could you give to each?") Yes I know, but if these are the facts, if attention is so important, then at some point the people who allot the money for schools and for training programmes must, quite simply, put it to themselves like this: children flourish if they are given attention—and their teachers' expectations that they will succeed. Therefore we must pay out enough money to the educators so that enough attention may be provided. . . .

Another range of experiments were carried out extensively in the United States, and for all I know, in Canada too. For instance, a team of doctors cause themselves to be admitted as patients into a mental hospital, unknown to the staff. At once they start exhibiting the symptoms expected of mentally ill people, and start behaving within the range of behaviour described as typical of mentally ill people. The real doctors all, without exception, say they are ill, and classify them in various ways according to the symptoms described by them. It is not the doctors or the nurses who see that these so-called ill people are quite normal; it is the other patients who see it. They aren't taken in; it is they who can see the truth. It is only with great difficulty that these well people convince the staff that they are well, and obtain their release from hospital.

Again: a group of ordinary citizens, researchers, cause themselves to be taken into prison, some as if they were ordinary prisoners, a few in the position of warders. Immediately both groups start behaving appropriately: those as warders begin behaving as if they were real warders, with authority, badly treating the prisoners, who for their part, show typical prison behaviour, become paranoid, suspicious, and so forth. Those in the role of warders confessed afterwards they could not prevent themselves enjoying the position of power, enjoying the sensation of controlling the weak. The so-called prisoners could not believe, once they were out, that they had in fact behaved as they had done.

But suppose this kind of thing were taught in schools?

Let us just suppose it, for a moment.... But at once the nub of the problem is laid bare.

Imagine us saying to children: "In the last fifty or so years, the human race has become aware of a great deal of information about its mechanisms; how it behaves, how it must behave under certain circumstances. If this is to be useful, you must learn to contemplate these rules calmly, dispassionately, disinterestedly, without emotion. It is information that will set people free from blind loyalties, obedience to slogans, rhetoric, leaders, group emotions." Well, there it is.

What government, anywhere in the world, will happily envisage its subjects learning to free themselves from governmental and state rhetoric and pressures? Passionate loyalty and subjection to group pressure is what every state relies on. Some, of course, more than others. Khomeini's Iran, and the extreme Islamic sects, the Communist countries, are at one end of the scale. Countries like Norway, whose national day is celebrated by groups of children in fancy dress carrying flowers, singing and dancing, with not a tank or a gun in sight, are at the other. It is interesting to speculate: what country, what nation, when, and where, would have undertaken a programme to teach its children to be people to resist rhetoric, to examine the mechanisms that govern them? I can think of only one—America at its birth, in that heady period of the Gettysburg Address. And that time could not have survived the Civil War, for when war starts, countries cannot afford disinterested examination of their behaviour. When a war starts, nations go mad—and have to go mad, in order to survive. When I look back at the Second World War, I see something I didn't more than dimly suspect at the time. It was that everyone was crazy. Even people not in the immediate arena of war. I am not talking of the aptitudes for killing, for destruction, which soldiers are taught as part of their training, but a kind of atmosphere, the invisible poison, which spreads everywhere. And then people everywhere begin behaving as they never could in peacetime. Afterwards we look back, amazed. Did I really do that? Believe that? Fall for that bit of propaganda? Think that all our enemies were evil? That all our own nation's acts were good? How could I have tolerated that state of mind, day after day, month after month—perpetually stimulated, perpetually whipped up into emotions that my mind was meanwhile quietly and desperately protesting against?

No, I cannot imagine any nation—or not for long—teaching its citizens to become individuals able to resist group pressures.

And no political party, either. I know a lot of people who are socialists of various kinds, and I try this subject out on them, saying: all governments these days use social psychologists, experts on crowd behaviour, and mob behaviour, to advise them. Elections are stage managed, public issues presented according to the rules of mass psychology. The military uses this information. Interrogators, secret services and the police use it. Yet these issues are never even discussed, as far as I am aware, by those parties and groups who claim to represent the people.

On one hand there are governments who manipulate, using expert knowledge and skills, on the other hand people who talk about democracy, freedom, liberty and all the rest of it, as if these values are created and maintained by simply talking about them, by repeating them often enough. How is it that so-called democratic movements don't make a point of instructing their members in the laws of crowd psychology, group psychology?

When I ask this, the response is always an uncomfortable, squeamish reluctance, as if the whole subject is really in very bad taste, unpleasant, irrelevant. As if it will all just go away if it is ignored.

So at the moment, if we look around the world, the paradox is that we may see this new information being eagerly studied by governments, the possessors and users of power—studied and put into effect. But the people who say they oppose tyranny literally don't want to know.

Laboratories of Social Change

In an earlier talk in this series I said that it was hard to see anything good and hopeful in a world that seems increasingly horrific. To listen to the news is enough to make you think you are living in a lunatic asylum.

But wait ... we all know the news is presented to us for maximum effect, that bad news seems, at least, to be more effective in arousing us than good news—which in itself is an interesting comment on the human condition. We are all regularly presented, day after day, with bad news, the worst, and I think our minds are more and more set into attitudes of foreboding and depression. But is it possible that all the bad things going on—and I don't have to list them, for we all know what they are—are a reaction, a dragging undertow, to a forward movement in the human social evolution that we can't easily see? Perhaps, looking back, let's say in a century or two centuries, is it possible people will say: "That was a time when extremes battled for supremacy. The human mind was developing very fast in the direction of self-knowledge, self-command, and as always happens, as always *has* to happen, this thrust forward aroused its opposite, the forces of stupidity, brutality, mob thinking"? I think it is possible. I think that this is what is happening.

Let us look at something that is extraordinarily encouraging. In the last twenty or so years quite a few countries that were dictatorships, tyrannies, have opted to become democracies. Among them are Greece, Portugal, Spain, Brazil and Argentina. Some of these are precarious—democracy is always precarious, and must be fought for. But countries that were in the grip of single-minded, simple-minded, stultifying systems of thought have chosen to attempt the more complicated, many-choiced balances of democracy.

In the balance against this hopeful fact, we must put a sad one, which is that large numbers of young people, when they reach the age of political activity, adopt a stance or an attitude that is very much part of our times. It is that democracy is only a cheat and a sham, only the mask for exploitation, and that they will have none of it. We have almost reached a point where if one values democracy, one is denounced as reactionary. I think that this will be one of the attitudes that will be found most fascinating to historians of the future. For one thing, the young people who cultivate this attitude towards democracy are usually those who have never experienced its opposite: people who've lived under tyranny, value democracy.

It is not that I don't understand it—I understand it only too well, having lived through the process myself. Democracy, liberty, fair play, and so forth—these have been stuffed down one's throat, and suddenly you see the most appalling injustices all around you, and shout: "Hypocrite!" In my case, it was Southern Rhodesia, where democracy was for the white minority, and the black majority had no rights of any kind. But when people are in that state of mind, what is forgotten is that a democracy, no matter how imperfect, offers the possibility of reform, change. It offers freedom of choice. It is this freedom to choose that is the new idea, historically speaking. I think we tend to forget how new these ideas are in that an individual should have rights, that a citizen should be able to criticize the government.

How new is it? When was this concept born into the human community for the first time? At this point, there are people who start muttering about ancient Greece, forgetting that it was a slave state that allowed certain minimal freedoms to a male minority. For argument's sake, it would be safe to say that our concepts of liberty, of the rights of the individual, were born in the English Revolution, in the French Revolution, and in the American Revolution. Very young ideas indeed. Very frail. Very precarious.

That an individual should be entitled to the rule of the law—why, three or four centuries ago, they wouldn't have known what you meant by it. Now it is an idea so powerful that strong and ruthless governments are brought down by it.

An idea seems to have taken root that there is such a thing as civilized government, even that there is a general consensus what civilized government is. How otherwise could the citizens of Argentina have agreed that they wanted to sue their deposed government for wicked and cruel behaviour? For improper behaviour? This seems to me the most extraordinary and encouraging thing—that it could be happening at all, proving to us all that in the world mind there *is* an idea of what government ought to be. Has there ever been an example before, of citizens wanting to sue a government for improper behaviour? I am no historian, but it does seem to me that this is a new thing in the world.

Yet I think we may very well see countries that take it for granted they are democracies losing sight of democracy, for we are living in a time when the great over-simplifiers are very powerful—communism, fundamentalist Islam. Poor economies breed tyrannies.

But good ideas don't get lost, though they may be submerged for a time.

An example. I have been talking about what we call the "soft sciences," social psychology, and social anthropology and the rest, and their contribution to understanding ourselves as social animals, and how these young sciences are denigrated, patronized, put down. As everybody knows, money is getting very short in Britain, university departments are closing, all kinds of studies are being cut. This type of a science has been badly affected, often the first to be cut—yet I have just read that in various universities, departments studying social psychology, social science and so forth have been reprieved, because of their usefulness to industry. In other words, they are proving their value where it counts.

Another example, not current, but one I believe will be in the future. Because communism has turned out so badly, proved itself not only one of the bloodiest tyrannies ever, but also so inefficient that any type of regime, no matter how bad, is preferred to it, we forget that communism was born out of the ancient dream of justice for everybody.

It is a very powerful dream, a powerful engine for social change. Because communism is at this present time equated with barbarism, inefficiency and tyranny, that doesn't mean that the idea of real justice will not be reborn.

Meanwhile there is no country in the world whose structure is not of a privileged class and a poor class. There is always a power elite with the mass of the people excluded from wealth and from any sort of political power.

In my more gloomy moments, I do brood about the fact that it took the Communists' Soviet Union only a couple of generations to develop a power elite as rich and as privileged as any in the world. Communist China is reported to be going the same way and so are some of the new African states. But if this is some kind of an inevitable process, for this time at least, that all types of society produce privileged elites, then at least we should acknowledge it and work for as much flexibility as possible inside the structure.

There is no group or party setting itself up against this state of affairs that does not see itself as an elite, whether it be the dictatorship of the proletariat, headed by the Communist party, or terrorist groups, or the political parties of the democracies, which by definition know what is best for everyone else.

Elites, privileged classes, groups better educated than others . . . this seems to be the stage at which the world is now, or at least, nothing else seems to be visible anywhere.

There are all kinds of elites, some retrograde and useless that only act as brakes on social change, while others, I believe, are productive. If I say that I think elites, privileged groups, are often useful, then that makes me reactionary, but it depends on who the elite is: as I said before, if you call it the vanguard of the proletariat, then that changes things, doesn't it? Or, if I say I think ginger groups, pressure groups, are invaluable because they prevent a society from going sleepy and unself-critical, then that is all right too—no, it is the word *elite* that is suspect. Very well, let's discard it: we live in a time when people may murder for the sake of a word, or a phrase. . . .

There is a certain social process that is known and very visible, but perhaps not acknowledged as much as it should be. It is that one where a new idea (or an old one in new form) is accepted by a minority, while the majority are shouting treason, rubbish, kook, Communist, capitalist, or whatever is the valued term of abuse in that society. The minority develop this idea, at first probably in secrecy, or semi-secrecy, and then more and more visibly, with more and more support until . . . guess what? This seditious, impossible, wrong-headed idea becomes what is known as "received opinion" and is loved and valued by the majority. Meanwhile, of course, a new idea, still seditious etc. and so forth, has been born some-where else, and is being cultivated and worked out by a minority. Suppose we redefine the word elite, for our present purposes, to mean any group of people who for any reason are in the possession of ideas that put them ahead of the majority?

When you get to my age—I was bound to say this at some point, you'll agree—when you get to my age, watching this process continuously at work in society is one of the more entertaining ways of passing one's time. It is an entertainment on the whole denied to all but a few of the more reflective young, because the young are still able to believe more easily in permanence. What! That the bunch of ideas *they* cherish are destined for the dustheap? Of course not!

But suppose we got to the point where at least enough of us could agree that this *is* a process continually at work —even in societies that outlaw new ideas, like the Com-munist ones—making it inevitable that today's treason is tomorrow's orthodoxy. Would that not make us more efficient than we are now, less punishing and bloody-minded, and ready to resist change? I think it would, and that there must come a point when this, like other mech-anisms in society, will be used, instead of resisted or ignored. They can be ignored only by people who do not study history.

Which brings me to another quite remarkable phe-nomenon of our times. It is that young people are not interested in history. In a recent survey in Britain, young people who were asked what they thought were useful subjects of study put history very low: only seven per cent saw any value in it. I think one reason for this is psychological, easy to see and to understand, particularly, again, if you've lived through that stage yourself. If you are self-consciously "young," and by definition progres-sive, or revolutionary or whatever, but in any case, in the right (young being against the old who are stupid and reactionary), then the last thing you want to do is to look at history, where you will learn that this attitude on the part of the young is perennial, part of a permanent social process. You do not want to read anything that upsets your view of yourself as a gloriously new and amazing phenomenon, whose ideas are fresh, in fact just minted, and probably by yourself, or at least, by your friends, or by the leader you revere, an altogether new unsullied creature destined to change the world. If I sound mocking, then I am only laughing at my own young self—but that is the point.

I think that this attitude, that history is not worth studying, will strike those who come after us as quite amazing.

After all, what we have seen since the French Revolution (some would say since the utopian and socialist groups of Cromwell's time) has amounted to a laboratory of experiment in different types of socialism, different types of society, from the thirteen-year-long war regime of Hitler, which called itself national socialism, to the Labour governments of Britain, from the Communist states of Russia and China, to Cuba, to Ethiopia, to Somalia, and on and on. You'd think that people dedicated to production of new types of society would fall on these examples, of what has actually happened, in order to study and learn from them.

I repeat: one way of looking at the last two and a half centuries, is that they have been laboratories of social change. But in order to learn from them one needs a certain distance, detachment; and it is precisely this detachment that makes possible, I believe, a step forward in social consciousness. One learns nothing, about anything, ever, when in a state of boiling ferment, or partisan enthusiasm.

I think children should be taught about history not as

is usually the case now, that this is the record of long past events, which one ought to know about for some reason or other. But that this is a story from which one may learn not only what has happened, but what may, and probably will, happen again.

Literature and history, these two great branches of human learning, records of human behaviour, human thought, are less and less valued by the young, and by educators, too. Yet from them one may learn how to be a citizen and a human being. We may learn how to look at ourselves and at the society we live in, in that calm, cool, critical and sceptical way which is the only possible stance for a civilized human being, or so have said all the philosophers and the sages.

But all the pressures go the other way, towards learning only what is immediately useful, what is functional. More and more the demand is for people to be educated to function in an almost certainly temporary stage of technology. Educated for the short term.

We have to look at the word *useful* again. In the long run what is useful is what survives, revives, comes to life in different contexts. It may look now as if people educated to use our newest technologies efficiently are the world's elite, but in the long run I believe that people educated to have, as well, that point of view that used to be described as humanistic—the long-term, over-all, contemplative point of view—will turn out to be more influential. Simply because they understand more of what is going on in the world. It is not that I undervalue the new technicians. On the contrary. It is only that what they know is by definition a temporary necessity.

To my mind the whole push and thrust and development of the world is towards the more complex, the flexible, the open-minded, the ability to entertain many ideas, sometimes contradictory ones, in one's mind at the same time.

We are seeing now an example of the price a society must pay for insisting on orthodox, simple-minded, slogan thinking: the Soviet Union is a creaking, anachronistic, inefficient, barbaric society, because its type of communism outlaws flexibility of thought. "Life itself"— to use the phrase the Communists like using—"life itself" is showing just what happens to societies that allow themselves to ossify in dead patterns of thought. (The new ruler Gorbachev is trying to remedy this.) We may observe how the Chinese, always a clever and pragmatic people, are allowing themselves to change. We may see how fundamentalist Islam creates societies that will, because of their inflexibility, soon be shown up for what they are, while other societies, more flexible, more open, race ahead.

In the long term, I think the race will go to the democracies, the flexible societies. I know that if one looks around the world at the moment, this may seem a rather over-optimistic view, particularly when we see that the new information about how we work and function is used so skillfully and cynically by governments, police departments, armies, secret services—all those functions of administration that can be used to diminish and control the individual.

But it is my belief that it is always the individual, in the long run, who will set the tone, provide the real development in a society.

It is not always easy to go on valuing the individual, when everywhere individuals are so put down, denigrated, swamped by mass thinking, mass movements and, on a smaller scale, by the group.

It is particularly hard for young people, faced with what seems like impervious walls of obstacles, to have belief in their ability to change things, to keep their personal and individual viewpoints intact. I remember very clearly how it seemed to me in my late teens and early twenties, seeing only what seemed to be impregnable systems of thought, of belief—governments that seemed unshakeable. But what has happened to those governments like the white government in Southern Rhodesia, for instance? To those powerful systems of faith, like the Nazis, or the Italian Fascists, or to Stalinism? To the British Empire ... to all the European empires in fact, so recently powerful? They have all gone, and in such a short time.

Looking back now, I no longer see these enormous blocs, nations, movements, systems, faiths, religions, but only individuals, people who when I was young I might have valued, but not with much belief in the possibility of their changing anything. Looking back, I see what a great influence an individual may have, even an apparently obscure person, living a small, quiet life. It is individuals who change societies, give birth to ideas, who, standing out against tides of opinion, change them. This is as true in open societies as it is in oppressive societies, but of course the casualty rate in the closed societies is higher. Everything that has ever happened to me has taught me to value the individual, the person who cultivates and preserves her or his own ways of thinking, who stands out against group thinking, group pressures. Or who conforming no more than is necessary to group pressures, quietly preserves individual thinking and development.

I am not at all talking about eccentrics, about whom such a fuss is made in Britain. I do think that only a very rigid and conforming society could have produced the idea of an eccentric in the first place. Eccentrics tend to be in love with the image of eccentricity, and once embarked on this path, become more and more picturesque, developing eccentricity for its own sake. No, I am talking about people who think about what is going on in the world, who try to assimilate information about our history, about how we behave and function—people who advance humanity as a whole.

It is my belief that an intelligent and forward-looking society would do everything possible to produce such individuals, instead of, as happens very often, suppressing them. But if governments, if cultures, don't encourage their production, then individuals and groups can and should.

We are back with the concept of an elite, and that is all right with me, in this context. We cannot expect a government to say to children something like this: "You are going to have to live in a world full of mass movements, both religious and political, mass ideas, mass cultures. Every hour of every day you will be deluged with ideas and opinions that are mass produced, and regurgitated, whose only real vitality comes from the power of the mob, slogans, pattern thinking. You are going to be pressured all through your life to join mass movements, and if you can resist this, you will be, every day, under pressure from various types of groups, often of your closest friends, to conform to them.

"It will seem to you many times in your life that there is no point in holding out against these pressures, that you are not strong enough.

"But you are going to be taught how to examine these mass ideas, these apparently irresistible pressures, taught how to think for yourself, and to choose for yourself.

"You will be taught to read history, so as to learn how short-lived ideas are, how apparently the most irresistible and persuasive ideas can, and do, vanish overnight. You will be taught how to read literature, which is the study of mankind by itself, so as to understand the development of people and peoples. Literature is a branch of anthropology, a branch of history; and we will make sure that you will know how to judge an idea from the point of view of long-term human memory. For literature and history are branches of human memory, recorded memory.

"To these studies will be added those new branches of information, the young sciences of psychology, social psychology, sociology and so on, so that you may understand your own behaviour, and the behaviour of the group which will be, all your life, both your comfort and your enemy, both your support and your greatest temptation, since to disagree with your friends—you group animal—will always be painful.

"You will be taught that no matter how much you have to conform outwardly—because the world you are going to live in often punishes unconformity with death —to keep your own being alive inwardly, your own judgement, your own thought. . . ."

Well, no, we cannot expect this kind of thing to be in the curriculum laid down by any state or government currently visible in the world. But parents may talk and teach like this, and certain schools may. And groups of young adults who have run the gauntlet of state education, or private education, and survived with enough of their critical faculties intact to want more than they have been given, may teach themselves and each other what they will.

Such people, such individuals, will be a most productive yeast and ferment, and lucky the society who has plenty of them.

We live in an open society. We pride ourselves on it, and so we should. An open society is distinguished by the fact that government may not keep information from its citizens, must allow the circulation of ideas. But what we have, we take for granted. What we are used to, we cease to value. Generations of our forebears fought for the freedom of ideas, so that we may have what we do have. One only has to meet people from behind the Iron Curtain, particularly from the Soviet Union, where ideas are not allowed to circulate, where information is suppressed, where there is a close, claustrophobic, oppressive atmosphere, to be reminded how very fortunate we are, even with all the defects our societies do have.

We are fortunate in that we are able to teach ourselves what we will, if our schools seem to us deficient; and to reach out anywhere at all for ideas that seem to us valuable.

I think that we should make more use of these freedoms than we do.

Casting about for an illustration of my belief that independent-minded and iconoclastic individuals can influence events, I chanced upon Akhnaten, the Egyptian ruler who came to the throne 1,400 years before Christ. The state religion was gloomy and death-ridden, and there were innumerable gods, half animal, half human. Akhnaten disliked this religion, so he threw out the gloomy oppressive priests, the gloomy half-animal gods, and adopted a cheerful religion, based on love, and a single god. His reign lasted for only a few years before he was overthrown; the old religion and the old priesthood returned. Akhnaten, if referred to at all, was called The Heretic, or the Great Criminal, he was made a non-person, as we say now. He disappeared from history, and only in the 19th century was his existence rediscovered. Since then he has had a quite extraordinary effect on all kinds of people. Freud believed that Moses got the idea of monotheism from the suppressed religion of Aten, Akhnaten's religion. More recently, Thomas Mann put this Akhnaten in his great novel, *Joseph And His Brethren*. Recently, Philip Glass has written an opera about him. What was he really like, this king who ruled 3,500 years ago, who has such a remarkable capacity to spark our imaginations? We know very little about him, except that he overthrew a set of ideas and imposed, however briefly, a new set of ideas. One single, brave individual, challenging a massive machinery of priesthood and state. One person, setting a religion of love, of light, against a religion of death. . . .

Very likely, when Akhnaten was a little boy, he said to himself, what can one person do against this awful, heavy, powerful, oppressive regime, with its priests and its frightening gods—what is the point of even trying?

By using our freedoms, I do not mean just joining demonstrations, political parties, and so on and so forth, which is only part of the democratic process, but examining ideas, from whatever source they come, to see how they may usefully contribute to our lives and to the societies we live in.